KIDS ASK™

What?

Illustrations by Linda Howard Bittner

Publications International, Ltd.

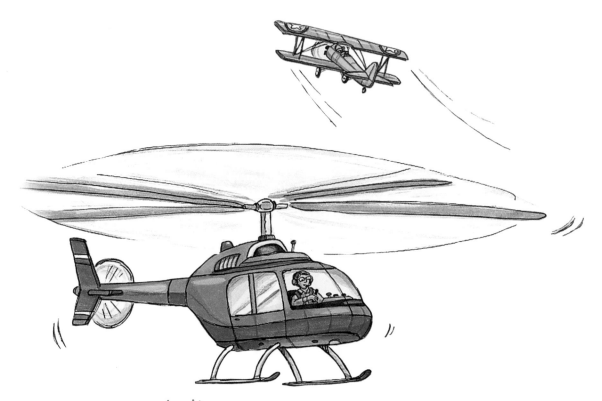

What makes a helicopter different from an airplane?

Contents

What is a seashell?

Shells that wash onto the beach are the empty shells of small sea creatures such as clams or oysters. These shells help protect the animals' soft bodies from the pounding surf and other sea creatures that might eat them.

What makes the sky so colorful at sunset?

The short answer is dirt. Can you believe it? The prettiest sunsets happen when clean air has small amounts of dust and water. These scatter light in all directions, making more red and yellow and less pink.

FUN FACT

Have you ever heard of a green flash? It's a flash of green light seen during the last few seconds of a sunset or sunrise. It's difficult to see a green flash because it happens so quickly. Don't ever look directly at the sun because it could damage your eyes.

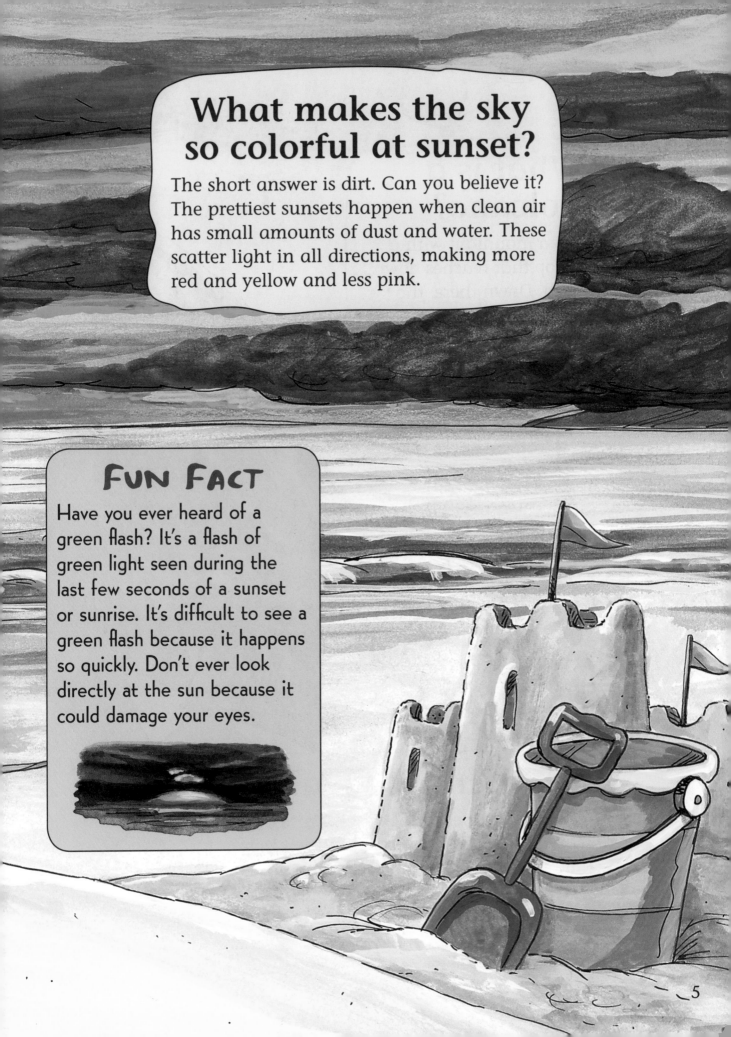

What is a volcano?

A volcano is a mountain with a hole in the top that reaches down into the earth. Down there, the temperature is hot enough to melt rock! When a volcano erupts, or explodes, the melted rock boils out.

What is lava?

Lava is the melted rock that comes out of a volcano when it erupts. When this happens, the lava runs down the sides of the volcano and moves slowly across the land. Lava burns everything in its path.

FUN FACT

The largest volcano on Earth is Mauna Loa on the island of Hawaii. It covers half of the island. It last erupted in 1984, and it may erupt again soon.

What are freckles?

Freckles are small, flat, tan or brown-colored cells in the skin. *Melanin* is a chemical in our bodies that determines our skin color. The body makes extra melanin when you spend time in the sun. This causes a suntan. But tanning isn't always even, and sometimes freckles are produced. Always wear sunscreen to help prevent a sunburn!

FUN FACT

Do you have curly hair or straight hair? Your hair type depends on the kind of hair your parents have. Hair can also change shape because of the weather. On a rainy day, straight hair may get a bit curly and curly hair can get very curly.

What makes people have different colors of skin?

People are people, no matter what they look like. There are many different colors of skin. A person's skin color depends on the color of his or her parents' skin. The amount of melanin you have determines how much protection you have from the sun and whether you have light or dark skin. People with light skin have less melanin. People with darker skin have more melanin.

What makes the moon shine?

The moon does not have light of its own like the sun does. The light we see from the moon is actually the light of the sun reflecting, or bouncing, off the moon's surface. So without the sun, we could not see the moon.

FUN FACT

Stars are huge balls of fire. A star begins as a cloud of dust and gases. These clouds get hotter and hotter as they swirl in space. When they flame and burn, a star is born!

What makes a rocket go?

To get into space, a rocket moves very fast and works like a jet engine. The rocket's engines burn thousands of gallons of fuel and make hot gases. These gases rush downward and push the rocket up.

What are mountains?

It can take thousands, or even millions, of years for a mountain to form. Most mountains were made from rock that was pushed up from the bottom of the oceans. Other mountains formed along cracks in the earth's surface. The land on either side of the crack was pushed up or down to form a mountain.

What is snow?

Snow is really just frozen rain. Droplets of water in a cloud form tiny ice crystals that become snowflakes. Because snow is mostly air, a very small amount of water makes a large amount of snow.

FUN FACT

Mount Everest is the highest mountain on Earth. Its peak is more than 29,000 feet above sea level. That's almost as high as a jet airplane flies! And Mount Everest is still growing! It grows almost one inch every year.

What does a bulldozer do?

Bulldozers do big jobs! A bulldozer has a big blade on its front to push heavy rocks and move big piles of dirt from place to place. Bulldozers also make the ground smooth.

FUN FACT

Some construction vehicles are driven from outside the vehicle, just like a remote-control car. Special bulldozers that work in the water are driven this way so nobody needs to get wet!

What does a crane do?

A crane is like a very long and strong arm. Some cranes have a big claw at the end that picks up dirt, rocks, and other things. Other cranes use a big hook at the end to move objects from place to place. Some cranes also have strong magnets for picking up metal objects.

What causes static electricity?

Static electricity is electricity that has built up on an object. It is caused by friction, or rubbing. If you're wearing socks and you rub your feet on a carpet and then touch a metal object, you will get a shock. You might even get a shock when you flip on a light switch or touch another person. This is caused by static electricity.

What makes a lightbulb light up?

Inside a lightbulb is a thin wire. Electricity makes this wire get very hot—so hot that it glows! This special kind of wire glows very brightly for a long time before it burns out.

What makes a surfboard go?

First, a surfer watches for a good wave. Then he paddles so that the surfboard is in front of where the wave curls over. As the wave rolls toward the shore, it pushes the surfer in front of it. A rudder on the bottom of the board helps the surfer steer.

What makes the ocean blue?

The water in the ocean is really clear, not blue. It only looks blue because the blue sky is reflected in the water. On a dark day, the ocean may look gray or even dark green.

FUN FACT

The blue whale is the biggest animal in the world. It can grow to be more than 100 feet long. That's longer than the distance between the bases on a baseball field! Blue whales can weigh more than 250,000 pounds. That's as much as 80 cars! They are also louder than a jet plane when they talk to each other.

What makes soda pop fizzy?

Soda pop is made with carbonated water. This is water that contains tiny air bubbles. When you open a can or bottle of soda pop, the *whoosh* sound you hear is the bubbles escaping. If you leave the bottle or can open, the bubbles will leak out and the soda pop will go "flat."

FUN FACT

People get hiccups when too much air gets into their lungs. The air hits the space around the lungs and moves the vocal cords. This makes the *hic* sound. Some people claim you can cure the hiccups by breathing into a paper bag.

What causes a burp?

A burp is nothing but gas. The air we breathe contains gases (but not the type of gas you put into a car). So when we eat or drink, we don't just swallow food or a liquid, we also swallow air and gases. But these gases need to get out of the body. When they escape through the mouth, we call it a burp. Cover your mouth when you burp, and be sure to say, "Excuse me."

What do penguins do to keep warm?

Penguins have a layer of fat called *blubber* that helps keep them warm. They also have two layers of feathers. These feathers are waterproof to help the penguins stay warm when they get out of the water. Penguins also huddle together in large groups to keep each other warm.

FUN FACT

Even though penguins are birds and have wings, they cannot fly. Penguins have small wings that work like paddles to help them swim faster.

What makes a helicopter different from an airplane?

Unlike an airplane, a helicopter doesn't need a long runway in order to take off. A helicopter can fly in almost any direction—straight up, backward, and even sideways. It can make sharper turns than an airplane can. It can also stay in the air over one spot. This is called *hovering*. A helicopter can even land on top of a building.

AIR SHOW TODAY

What is a blimp?

Blimps, or airships, are often seen floating over sports games and other big events. They are like giant balloons filled with a type of gas that is lighter than air. Heavy bags of sand or water keep the blimp on the ground. To send it up in the air, the bags are released. To bring it down, gas is let out of the blimp. Engines and propellers move the blimp through the sky.

FUN FACT

Have you ever felt your ears "pop"? When you ride in an airplane or in the elevator of a tall building, your ears may pop. This happens because as you go up (or down), the air around you presses on your ears. As your ears get used to the pressing air, you feel a pop.

What happens when bears sleep?

Bears sleep, or hibernate, for about six months of the year when their food becomes scarce. While they are hibernating from October to April, they do not eat or drink. Bears use the fat stored in their bodies for food. They choose a cave or a hollow log or dig a hole for a place to sleep. Their hearts and lungs work very slowly while they hibernate.

What makes a skunk stink?

When skunks get scared, they do a little dance as a warning. If this doesn't scare the person or animal away, skunks have a secret weapon. Under their tails, skunks have two little sacs that contain an oily liquid. This liquid smells awful. If it gets on the skin or in the eyes, it can burn or even cause blindness. The smell can last for days—or even weeks. So if you see a skunk dance, run away!

What are goose bumps?

People get goose bumps when they feel cold or scared. When this happens, the tiny muscles in the skin around a piece of hair pull in. This causes the little bumps we call goose bumps. They most often form on the arms and legs.

FLAVOR OF THE MONTH
Rocky Road

What causes my stomach to growl?

The stomach is a very powerful muscle that grinds food and pushes it where it can be used by the body. You might hear it "growl" when you haven't eaten in a while. This is the sound of your stomach mashing the little bit of food and air that are left inside of it. It is trying to tell you that you should eat something soon.

Grrr...!

What makes a cat's eyes glow in the dark?

A cat has special parts in the back of its eyes. These parts are like mirrors. When light shines into a cat's eyes, it bounces off these parts. This fills the cat's eyes with light. Cats can see things at night that people cannot.

FUN FACT

The largest dog ever known was an Old English Mastiff named Zorba. Zorba was more than 8 feet long from nose to tail and weighed 343 pounds. That's as much as two grown men!

What do dogs dream about?

Because dogs can't talk, nobody knows for sure what they dream about. But scientists are sure that dogs dream, just as humans do. They even have scary dreams.

What makes the colors of a rainbow?

It takes two things to make a rainbow: sunlight and raindrops. Sunlight is made up of red, orange, yellow, green, blue, indigo (dark blue), and violet-colored light. When the sun shines through the raindrops in just the right way, we see beautiful colors against the clouds.